The Lorette Wilmot Library
and Media Center
Nazareth College of Rochester

WALTER VANDYKE BINGHAM

HOMO SAPIENS AUDUBONIENSIS

A TRIBUTE TO

Walter VanDyke Bingham

Millicent Todd Bingham

THE NATIONAL AUDUBON SOCIETY
NEW YORK · 1953

PRINTED BY
THE ANTHOENSEN PRESS, PORTLAND, MAINE, U.S.A.

Foreword

The members of the staff and the students at the Audubon Camp here in the Todd Wildlife Sanctuary on Hog Island in Muscongus Bay, Maine, have just suffered a grievous loss. For on the seventh of this month Walter Bingham died of a heart attack.

In his profession, that of scientific psychology applied to human betterment, Walter Bingham was a leader. But although not primarily a student of the natural world, he has influenced the destiny of this island since first its mission was glimpsed more than twenty years ago. His analysis of traits of a naturalist, in an article entitled Homo sapiens auduboniensis, *has been so helpful to our students in identifying at an early age promising recruits for the out-of-doors professions that we could think of no better tribute to his memory than to continue its usefulness in more permanent form.*

But this article is a small part of what he has done for us here. It is not too much to say that his belief in our Camp and what it stands for has from the beginning sustained us all. His love of this place, his eagerness to put at the disposal of those who come here any knowledge or skills he possessed, have made him so much a part of our work that we want to put into words for those who did not know him, and for those who did, some of his more noticeable characteristics.

To present the article he wrote for us and to tell us what manner of man he was we have asked his wife, Millicent Todd Bingham, to write the introduction to this, our tribute to a dear and honored friend.

For the National Audubon Society

JOHN H. BAKER, *President*
CARL W. BUCHHEISTER, *Vice President and Director, Audubon Camp of Maine*

Audubon Camp of Maine
July, 1952

Beyond Psychology

by

MILLICENT TODD BINGHAM

W ALTER BINGHAM was born on October 20, 1880, in Swan Lake,
a tiny hamlet near the Minnesota border in western Iowa.
His father and mother had actually gone there in a covered wagon.
They broke new ground and under God's guidance fashioned their
lives there, on the open prairie. In Walter's childhood swans inhab-
ited the shores of the lake and Indians bringing skins of wild creatures to sell for a few cents apiece came to his father's door. The in-
trepid spirit of those God-fearing Puritan pioneers shone through
his own fearless nature, illuminating the vision which led his profession into fields of usefulness untried before. The pioneer spirit
was in his blood, but the territory which he explored was that of the
mind of man. It is fortunate that he has left an account of his boyhood for in it can be seen the traits which have shaped the course of
his science and through it, by his contributions in two world wars,
the destinies of nations.

The first steps in his choice of a lifework are outlined in an article
entitled, "Try-Out Experiences of a Small-Town Boy," published
in the *Vocational Guidance Magazine*, March, 1940. He says, "In the
unfolding drama of self-discovery the occupational tryout played
a leading rôle. Sampling varied employments while still a school-
boy, I learned about my own capacities and preferences. . . .

"We small-town boys were always finding ways of trying ourselves
out. We sampled activities more varied than ordinarily come to the
city boy living in an apartment where it is not he but the janitor
who mends the doorbell, putties the broken windowpane, replaces
a worn washer in the faucet, and tends the furnace. . . . So we man-
aged to get along pretty well without benefit of organized vocational
guidance. We learned about our capacities and interests by actually
sampling a diversity of occupations; and one of us found, through

this gateway, an entrance to a rewarding career in industrial psychology."

Walter's curiosity about the world around him and his eagerness to understand everything he saw, a dominant trait throughout his life, appears in this account of his early years. His way of attacking a problem is illustrated by the following anecdote.

Why does the full moon look so big and so near when first it peeks over the eastern horizon? I must have been about fourteen when some of us boys began to argue about that venerable problem. One of us maintained that the newly risen moon appeared huge because it is seen right in among the sheds and trees and corn shocks. That makes it seem a lot nearer and so, big. This struck me as plausible until I noticed that the newly risen moon seemed as huge as ever when there were no barns or haystacks in sight, but only the flat blackness of the Iowa prairie. And anyhow, if the moon isn't nearer but only seems to be, it ought to look smaller instead of bigger.

Well, then, perhaps it actually is bigger in the sense that its rays have to pass through a great deal more atmosphere than they do an hour later. Suppose that the layers of air bend the rays, so that they are more nearly parallel with the curved surface of the earth; then those from the lower edge of the moon are refracted more than those from its top. In that case the picture a newly risen moon makes on the retina is really larger. "Let's find out," I proposed. "Tonight is full moon. We can stick a dime on the windowpane and measure how far away we have to get before the dime barely covers the moon's face. Then after an hour, we'll find out how much farther away we have to get."

That evening, with a ten-cent piece, a bamboo fishpole and a yardstick, we undertook to settle a psychological controversy by measurement. We tried to satisfy ourselves as to whether atmospheric refraction was operating in the way we thought it might. For the dime barely to eclipse the newly risen moon, one of us found that his eye had to be an inch or so nearer the window than it did an hour later, under the atmospheric conditions then prevailing. The rest of us were not entirely convinced. And in any event, how could so tiny a change produce so great a difference in appearance? There must be more to it than meets the eye. Is a newly risen moon more interesting, perhaps? More a part of our own surroundings? More friendly? We were baffled, and turned to something a great deal easier, namely the originals in Wentworth's Geometry. Those mathematical puzzles were as fascinating as chess.

This delight in solving "originals" in geometry helped Walter to find ways of conquering more difficult problems. Even as a boy, if confronted by a disagreeable fact which could be corrected he did not ask advice about what to do but tackled it instead, as the following incident will show.

One day not long after his voice had changed his grandmother said, "Walter, you talk through your nose. You don't want to go through life with a nasal voice do you?" He had never thought about it before, but now that she mentioned it he realized that his voice was pinched and it was nasal. Without saying anything he began to change his way of speaking and little by little re-placed his voice at a lower pitch. How well he succeeded everyone who heard his deep, vibrant voice will remember. Without being loud it had a carrying quality especially effective over the radio, helped of course by clean-cut enunciation. In the early days of broadcasting I remember his amusement when offered a lucrative position as a studio announcer!

Walter's undergraduate days spent at Beloit College, Wisconsin, where he graduated in 1901, were followed by four years of teaching in secondary schools in order to earn the money to pay for his college education. He taught several subjects, among them mathematics, geology and physiography. The problems of geography, my own field, never ceased to challenge him. One of its aims is to explain how the landscape has come to look as it does. Last summer we went to Norway and Sweden to attend two psychological congresses. Walter's analysis of the geological processes which had formed a region new to us, and his speculations as to the movements of the glaciers responsible for many of the landforms in Scandinavia, were far more ingenious than those of the geographer whose business it was to explain such things. Beginning as a teacher of physical science he left it, as he said, to tackle something harder, the study of the human mind.

In the fall of 1905 Walter entered the University of Chicago to study psychology in the laboratory of James Rowland Angell. Philosophy was a required "minor." So for one year he went to Harvard, then without rival in that field, where his thinking was guided by the great Josiah Royce. William James, too, he knew well. In Professor James's house on Irving Street he used to sit on the floor in front of the open fire with a group of eager students while they discussed the basic problems of human nature. It was a provocative year. Münsterberg fired his imagination as he speculated about psychology applied to industry, while Santayana was illustrating in his lectures the value of an immaculate delivery. From George Herbert Palmer, philosopher, Greek scholar and translator of the *Odyssey*, peerless teacher and author of *Self-cultivation in English,* Walter learned much about clearness of expression which he considered a first requirement for an educated man. He always insisted that his own ability in writing was uninspired, the result of gruelling effort; and he quoted Professor Palmer, "easy writing makes hard reading." But, as in everything he did, Walter Bingham's standards were so exacting that he sometimes rewrote a sentence ten times before he was satisfied to leave it. Professor Palmer was our dear friend. Each summer he handed over to us his venerable house in the Yard when Walter was teaching in the Harvard Summer School.

Greek philosophy had gripped Walter's attention at an early age. He says, "The hero of my boyhood was not Kit Carson, but the teacher, Socrates. Indeed my high school commencement oration [at the age of sixteen] was about that hero—a study built on readings in Jowett's *Plato* and Chambers' *Encyclopedia* which graced the middle shelf of our family library. To this day I cannot read without a lump in my throat the final pages of the *Symposium* which record the supreme tribute paid by the drunken rapscallion, Alcibiades, to his beloved teacher."

Next to philosophy I think Walter cared for music. How close it was to his heart is shown by a chance remark, that had he not chosen psychology as a career he would have liked to be the conductor of a symphony orchestra. In addition to a fine musical discrimination he had absolute pitch. It was natural that when the time came to select a subject for his doctoral dissertation he chose a problem at the point of intersection between his interest in psychological experimentation and his love of music—the nature of melody. Why, he asked, is one succession of notes a melody while a slight rearrangement of the same sounds is not, only "a tonal sequence without unity, without proper beginning or middle or end."

Always his greatest relaxation was in listening to music, the very best music—great orchestras, soloists and, during the last few years, the incomparable recitals of the Budapest String Quartet at the Library of Congress. Throughout the years when we lived in New York we attended three series of orchestral concerts, two of them under Toscanini. Walter understood the requirements and the limitations of the different instruments of an orchestra, and it was a privilege as well as great fun to sit beside him at a concert, for he could explain why a theme had been given to the English horn rather than to the oboe. He loved to speculate as to why the composer used the bassoon for a certain passage rather than the bass clarinet. This critical faculty was a result not only of his early psychological experiments with melody, and he became a musicologist of some standing, but because as a boy in western Iowa he had played *at* every instrument he could lay his hands on to see how it worked. He even tried the French horn with its fine adjustments of hand as well as lips, and could sympathetically applaud the proficiency of the solo horn who navigated through the shoals of a difficult passage without cracking.

Musical therapy, too, was of interest to Walter for in it he recognized an opportunity for scientific investigation. But he challenged the vague use of the term. Music will help to cure, yes, but what patients? And what music? At what level of taste both as to composition and as to performance?

In Berlin during the summer of 1907 he studied with Erich von Hornbostel, the eminent German musicologist, whom he had piloted about Chicago two years earlier. He liked to recall the great German's amazement at the virtuosity of the Chicago orchestra which he called "so virtuous." Another source of wonder to von Hornbostel was the fact that Walter greeted the hat clerk at the Auditorium. He happened to be a fellow student. Von Hornbostel was startled. No student in a German university would do such a thing. Walter explained that he himself had taken charge of the cloak room in order to be able to hear the concerts under Frederick Stock free of charge. In this simple episode von Hornbostel gained a glimpse of an unfamiliar social order.

The University of Chicago convocation in 1908 at which Walter received his doctor's degree provided an unexpected illustration of his musical versatility. The Alice Freeman Palmer chimes in the tower not far from the assembly hall had been recently installed. Just as the great audience was assembling it was discovered that the organ was out of order. Walter was standing in the academic procession about to move toward the stage when the secretary of the president hurried up to him and whispered, "Can you play the Convocation hymn on the chimes?" "Never have," said Walter. "Do you think you could?" "I could try," he said. In a piece of speedy organization which could only be called sleight of hand, a relay of scouts was stationed at intervals from the hall to within sight of Walter who had scurried up to the top of the bell tower. At the proper instant the signal was passed along, the audience awaiting the opening notes of the hymn rose to sing, but instead of the customary peal of the organ the melody rang out from the newly christened chimes. The audience caught its breath as the eerie beauty of the familiar tune resounded from an unfamiliar quarter. It is said to have given an original and memorable touch to that ceremony.

After receiving his doctorate in 1908 Walter became assistant to Professor Edward L. Thorndike at Teachers College, Columbia University, where he remained for two years. In view of the present proliferation of psychologists—there are now more than 11,000 members of the American Psychological Association—Walter often recalled the days when in 1910 he was its secretary and the total membership in the United States was 222. All were teachers and research workers in universities and colleges, busy instructing others how to become scholars and teachers of "pure" science. He too began as an experimentalist in "pure" science.

Associated with his investigation of the measurable sound waves of melody was his interest in prosody and poetics. He had a sure ear for cadence and emphasis, and a sure eye for length of line and the structure of stanzas. This was to be of immeasurable help to me in editing a volume of the unpublished poems of Emily Dickinson. Wherever my interest crossed a need, there his effort was expended. His knowledge of the more technical aspects of poetry was related to his interest in the process of creation. Amy Lowell was our friend. During the summers when Walter was teaching at Harvard we often dined at her home in Brookline. Sometimes, as I listened at a little distance, they would discuss the birth and the growth of a poem until two in the morning. After one such séance, in which he had tried to persuade her to save the first drafts of her poems in the interest of an investigation into the creative process, she wrote a poem entitled, when first she read it to us, "To the Impudent Psychologist." As posthumously published, however, the title is different— "To a Gentleman who wanted to see the first drafts of my poems in the interest of psychological research into the workings of the creative mind." But none of her first drafts were ever found. In parenthesis, Walter approached her mental processes from another angle too, by means of word-association tests, and found that she gave a higher proportion of unique responses than those of anyone outside a mental institution. The results of that discovery were never evaluated.

Before leaving the field of aesthetic experience I should mention one lowlier form of enjoyment. Walter's delight in fine music and in great literature was matched by his pleasure in a new sensation of taste or smell. He was fond of telling about his first encounter with crème de menthe. In a Chicago restaurant as a graduate student he was ordering unfamiliar dishes, food and drink he had never before heard of, to see what they were like. Among them was crème de menthe. When the waiter asked, "Green or white, sir," Walter replied promptly, "Green, please," although he had no idea what to expect. When he sipped the first drop he experienced a feeling of delicious pleasure. He was filled with "a precious essence," as Marcel Proust described an unfamiliar taste sensation. This delight Walter seemed to recapture each time as, with a beatific expression, he related the incident.

Though his approach to any problem was always that of a scientist, as severe in his demands as any student of psychometrics could wish, his intellect was but the tool of a compassionate heart. By a flash of insight he seemed to understand the troubles of other people and his deepest wish was to be able to help them. This was apparent before his scientific equipment was perfected. While at work in Angell's laboratory on the physics of sound, a tonal sequence and its interpretation as a melody, he spent an evening a week rehearsing a boys' orchestra at the University of Chicago Settlement back of the stockyards. In recalling that experience he remarked with a chuckle that the prime requisite for membership was not, however, a high average in tests of musical aptitude. Again, while acting as Professor Thorndike's assistant at Columbia University, Walter established a day nursery in the slums not far from his office.

This first teaching job convinced him of the importance of psychological tools in education. By means of them he found satisfaction in bringing others to their own best self-realization or, if you will, in providing the spark to galvanize them, though he would not have put it that way. Here then was to be his lifework—the application of his science to clarify human problems and, in particular, the devising of new tools for the purpose. He enjoyed statistics and was mechanically ingenious, delighting in apparatus of all kinds.

In 1910 Walter left Columbia to become head of the Department of Psychology at Dartmouth College. But the laboratory was not enough. It was not long before his scientific experimentation came to grips with his basic need, to be of help. First, it was the stammering son of a fellow-teacher, and the clumsy reading habits of another child, both of whom were cured by the aid of his self-invented psychological tools. But he was most interested in focusing toward productive channels the intellectual powers of the brilliant and able men in his classes. He never tired of relating the spectacular mathematical and statistical feats of one youthful undergraduate, Beardsley Ruml, for whom he later opened the way toward a brilliant career. Another gifted undergraduate wanted to be a dentist but had been discouraged from making the attempt because he was left-handed. Dentists' tools were made for right-handed people. Walter tested him for finger dexterity and coördination and proved to the student's satisfaction that he did better with his non-preferred right hand than most right-handed persons. Thus encouraged, the young man went on to achieve his heart's desire, eventually becoming Dean of the Harvard Dental School. To help other people to reach their objectives was always Walter's endeavor. Indeed, I have sometimes felt that his only pride was in the achievements of others.

Opportunities for significant service increased with the years: whether it was to help a bewildered policy maker or a floundering student; or to reduce a high accident rate in a metropolitan street railway system involving loss of jobs for the workers which he knew was unnecessary; or to correct the clumsily written presentation of an argument by a fellow psychologist—for he was an accomplished editor—or to guide a scientist from South Africa who was planning to introduce American methods into the industrial plants of his country. Walter's last piece of professional writing was a brief introduction to a book on that subject by A. G. Arbous of Johannesburg.

In 1915 Walter left the congenial academic seclusion of Dartmouth College to inaugurate an experiment, the application of psychology to practical problems, in a young institution, Carnegie Institute of Technology in Pittsburgh. The influence of that experiment upon the development of industrial psychology in this country is at the moment being traced by Dr. Leonard Ferguson in a detailed investigation. The pioneer Pittsburgh experiments and their verified results were soon to be of national importance in helping to win the First World War. For to the Army in 1917 was "sold" the totally new idea of classifying the soldiers so that their special skills could be discovered and used to the advantage not only of the individual fighting man but to the attainment of the objectives of the Army. Again from 1940 to 1947, as Chief Psychologist, Walter Bingham thought through and supervised this same branch of work for the Army to such effect that The Adjutant General has recently referred to him as the "architect of the classification system of the United States Army."

Walter's intellectual development is outlined in a sketch he wrote for Volume IV of *A History of Psychology in Autobiography* just published (August, 1952). It shows why his lifework followed the course it did. But his professional achievements, far-reaching though they were, do not explain the extent of his influence; nor was it his wide-ranging mind, the breadth of his interests and of his knowledge; nor even his clear thinking and its equally clear expression which many a time resolved a tangled situation for a fellow psychologist. The explanation lies deeper than any of these. For it was as a person that he touched both great and small. He believed in people, and felt a deference toward them so all-including that it often provoked me. In a social gathering he could appear quite unresponsive. I have seen him sit through an entire dinner-party at which we were guests of honor without saying one word. I used to tell him that he had no sense of responsibility for keeping up his end, for making the party a success. He would reply that he was so enjoying the wit of the others that he did not want to interrupt. I was sometimes exasperated, too, in a mixed gathering to see him sit quietly listening to a voluble—or is the proper term "verbalistic"—colleague as he expounded a topic on which Walter was an authority, without correcting what I knew to be a misstatement. Never mind. It was all a part of his consideration for others. As with Immanuel Kant, to Walter Bingham a human being was an end, never a means. Nothing rejoiced him like seeing a man attain his objective when he himself had been instrumental in making it possible. In one or two instances the ruthless way in which his generosity was taken advantage of made me indignant. But not Walter. He found only satisfaction in the knowledge that yet another man had been helped to reach the niche where he belonged.

I am trying to draw attention to certain sides of my husband's nature which of necessity are missing from a professional biography, although they are precisely the ones which had the widest influence and which perhaps contributed most to the richness and enjoyment of his many-sided life. His sunny temperament, his bright smile, his kindness, his humor and his courtesy, his perception of another's need and his prompt effort to help toward its fulfillment, these were combined with an unawareness of self and an indifference to self-interest so genuine that it identified his own happiness with the accomplishments of others. Which leads me to the point of my narrative—what he did for us here.

In 1936 the National Audubon Society started an experiment. Here on our forest-covered island in June of that year the first Audubon Camp for Adult Leaders was opened—for teachers, scout leaders, vocational counselors, those in the out-of-doors professions and many others. Located on the northern point of the island, it was separated from our own camp by a trackless mile of spruce and balsam forest interspersed with thickets of bayberry and raspberry bushes. But by water it was reached by a short row through the Narrows and across the head of the cove. After the close of the first season I wrote an article from which I quote. It was entitled, "Rescuing an Island—The struggle to preserve a piece of untouched wilderness off the coast of Maine as a wild life sanctuary and a nature camp dedicated to conservation."

In Muscongus Bay, paralleling the shore, looms the long dark outline of Hog Island—three hundred and thirty acres of untouched wilderness. It is roughly a mile and a half in length, half a mile wide, and at the northern end is separated by only a few minutes' row from the mainland. Ninety feet in height at the highest point, it is covered with dense forests of pine, spruce and balsam. Here and there, between two rocky points, a spring of clear water overflows across a little crescent beach. The granite ledges of which the island is built crop out along the bare crest. Into the shade of the sweet-smelling balsam woods below the botanist is lured by deep moss and beds of ferns. In June, lady's slippers and the faintly perfumed twin bells of *Linnea borealis* blossom in the shade, to be followed later in the summer by multi-colored mushrooms and the spectral Indian pipe.

As with most enterprises there is, back of the Hog Island experiment, a personal story. It falls roughly into three parts: First, a long period of years during which the island was cherished in its primitive state—a period of incubation for an idea. Four years ago that period came to an end in a sudden catastrophic event—an event which ushered in the second period, one of effort in trying to find some way by which the island could not only be preserved as a wildlife sanctuary, but utilized also for the advancement of knowledge concerning the wilderness and the life teeming within it. That goal reached, the third period opened with the establishment in June, 1936, of the first Audubon Nature Camp for Adult Leaders.

The narrative begins when, in the summer of 1908, my father and mother made a visit to Hog Island while cruising along the coast of Maine. My father, David Todd, was for thirty-six years Professor of Astronomy at Amherst College. My mother, Mabel Loomis Todd, a woman of varied interests and accomplishments—artistic, literary, civic, social—cared most of all about the world of nature, particularly about the preservation of forests and their wild inhabitants.

The first part of the story covers almost a quarter of a century, from 1908, when my mother first saw the island, until her death here on October 14, 1932. She was the real rescuer of Hog Island and to commemorate her success throughout those years in saving it from fire, from wood choppers and from other predators, it has been named the Todd Wildlife Sanctuary. During our first summer at the island we camped in tents near the water on the west shore where there was a shack, used by lobstermen and clam diggers, which we turned into our kitchen. We built a temporary shelter near the old cellar hole beyond and planned the buildings which, by 1920, amounted to seven in number.

WALTER BINGHAM, CAPTAIN OF THE "TAKUSAN"

WALTER BINGHAM INVESTIGATES A LARGE MUSHROOM WHICH,
OVERNIGHT, HAS BURST FULL GROWN THROUGH A COMPACT
HUMMOCK OF PIN CUSHION MOSS

My parents and I were interested in various aspects of nature. My father observed the heavens through a little telescope set up on our pier on starry nights. He wrote a book at the island, *Astronomy, Science of the Heavenly Bodies*. My mother studied the flowers, ferns and mushrooms. Her last piece of literary work, too, was finished at the island in 1931—re-editing her *Letters of Emily Dickinson,* first published in 1894. She wrote little articles about the spiders and cobwebs, the mosses and periwinkles, and was completing a book called *The Epic of Hog* at the time of her death. I was interested in the birds and in the physiography of the region—"the meaning of the landscape" as that science has been described.

In 1920 for the first time Walter VanDyke Bingham came to the island as our guest. A psychologist, he was suddenly plunged into a group of persons interested primarily in the world of nature. One of his most engaging traits was his ready response to a novel situation. His curiosity was instantly aroused by a point of view new to him. For the moment mysteries of the wilderness absorbed the attention of this student of the mysteries of the human mind.

Walter soon found ways in which to add to our pleasure and comfort. One of the first things about him which filled me with admiration was his success in building a fire out of wet logs. Stepping out of a group of friends who had come for a clambake on our beach but were about to pack up their baskets and go home when it began to drizzle, he selected the right sticks from a pile of driftwood which had been gathered for the purpose, and built so hot a fire that the clambake was completed as planned. And then, when the fog lifted as the sun set and the moon rose above the tree tops, he sang us a ballad of the old woman and the mill which he had learned as a young man from the lumberjacks in the great woods of Wisconsin. Everybody went home in high spirits forgetting that it had ever rained at all.

In December of that year we were married, and spent the following summer at the island.

Living in the wilderness in a camp without running water is a challenge to ingenuity. Walter found it so, and at once brought into play skills and knowledge he had not used since boyhood. He found scope for the exercise of his inventiveness in cutting down the tall dead trees in danger of falling on our camp buildings. With block and tackle firmly attached to his waist he would climb 20 or 30 feet up the trunk of a towering spruce, make the rope fast and clamber down again. Then, at one end of his treasured cross-cut saw, he would cut through the trunk near the ground just far enough to make the giant fall away from the house. When the tree coöperated as planned his smile of satisfaction would have graced the successful launching of a formula for a new test of aptitude. The job was completed by maneuvering the great trunk into position with a cant hook so that it could be sawn up and carried in to our fireplace for a cheerful blaze when the fog rolled in off the ocean.

Walter was much interested in the succession of growing things around him, the decay of one plant furnishing the necessary life-elements of another, the building of life out of death, as he wrote to his brother in California:

We think about you often here in the depths of the forest, a luxuriant forest that keeps reaching upward and spreading thicker over tracts that once were open to the sun. It has become more of an undertaking than once it was to make one's way among the spruce and balsam branches. Fallen giants too are more numerous, criss-crossed like jack-straws when winter storms raged, now from the northeast, now from the west.

How prolific is the forest to replace—yes, to anticipate—the ripe decline of its giants! Seedlings by the thousands send up candidates for maturity. Hundreds reach a youthful height of ten or twenty feet before succumbing to the stresses of competition, and shedding all their green as every branch and tiny twig takes on the rigor of black death. Only the fitted grasp the sunlight, keep flexible, and climb on, to heights of fifty, seventy, ninety feet.

When his friend Dr. F. Lyman Wells came to see us their talks by the fire sometimes turned from the profound problems of psychological science to Dr. Wells's hobby, the behavior of spiders. He has written many learned articles on the subject. He used to bring with him a tuning fork to the vibrations of which a spider will instantly respond although a touch on his web, or a flash of light from a sun glass leaves him motionless. Measurement of vibration had been a part of Walter's early studies in music, so the response to invisible sound waves on the part of the "noiseless patient spider" excited his curiosity. His knowledge of vibration was further challenged by watching a hermit thrush in full song whose highest notes he could not catch as they are beyond the range of human hearing.

Another phase of island life kindled his interest—heron rookeries. Previous to 1936 we had one on the island, half a mile or more south of our camp. When first we could catch their distant cackle as we hacked our way toward it through the unbroken forest his pace would quicken. And then, close, but just out of their sight as he perched on a ledge, he would observe the group behavior of a half a hundred or more great blue herons nesting in the tops of the spruce trees, their feeding habits and the plight of the weaker, more helpless nestlings.

Walter always enjoyed puzzles and meticulous measurement. The harder the problem the more was his interest challenged. This applied to puzzles, both intellectual and mechanical, as well as to chess and even bridge when the game was worth it. One day I asked him to tack the four quadrangles of the U. S. Geological Survey covering this region on the wall for ready reference. Due to the curvature of the earth's surface, observable in even so limited an area, the edges did not of course exactly match. The maps had to be trimmed and scrupulously fitted together. With rule and compass Walter went to work, paring off the minute deviations in such a way that when completed only an expert in surface mapping could note the discrepancies.

Mechanical devices were as familiar to him as the songs of birds to me. He supervised the building of our pier and runways. He took part in my father's engineering feats in moving stones off our beach: a scaffolding was so contrived beneath a large boulder that it would float at high tide and could be maneuvered to clear the beach for the dories.

But Walter's chief pleasure at the island, I think, was acting as skipper of our shining double-planked mahogany motor-boat, the *Takusan,* gift of an affluent friend. One memorable July day he piloted a group of friends out toward the open ocean where a gam of whales was rolling and tossing in what our friends described as frightening sport. They loomed perilously close to the boat, not half their size. Walter relished the adventure and described it for his brother:

Yesterday afternoon we went after whales as planned. Following a forenoon spent in drafting a book review of Dean Seashore's *A Preview to College and Life*—a little volume which will delight and stimulate both you and your boys—I rowed over to the sheltered spot where the *Takusan* was riding at her mooring, tightened the nuts which hold the head of the stuffing-box around the propeller-shaft, tuned up the engine, fed twenty gallons of gas into the tank and took a short run to Medomak public landing with Thomas Eliot, our Harvard Freshman cook—one of the National Scholarship boys—who trudged up the hill to Osier's country store for . . . the makings of a picnic supper. . . .*

It was fully 4:30 when we actually weighed anchor and headed for the South Seas—some ten miles south—where returned explorers reported having sighted whale yesterday forenoon. . . . We set our course southwestward, back across the Sound toward the quaint harbor called Round Pond (accent on the first syllable, pronounced "raound"). Thence we headed almost due south past Poland North Ledge, Poland South Ledge, Brown's Cove and Brown's Head, in a deep channel close to the rocky shores of the mainland. . . . Now well out toward open ocean, with nothing between us and the Guianas except Monhegan Island, scarcely discernible on the horizon, we kept sharp lookout in all directions. Occasionally a wave would slap the *Takusan*'s bow, splashing our cheeks with salt spray; but it was a joy to see how jauntily our little ship tossed these waters aside and how gracefully she rode the crests and troughs of the larger swells.

* Several omitted paragraphs have to do with the members of the "crew" including two "seasoned seaman from Muscongus Island." The latter were dropped off, however, at their home port about two miles to the south.

The temptation to yell "Thar she blows!" had to be resisted as from time to time we caught sight of a distant mound of spray made by the waves breaking over Brown's Head Ledge, Webber's Sunken Ledge, or some other distant point dangerous to mariners who might be caught in a fog. Southward our course continued toward a great red iron bell-buoy, which jangles monotonously to tell the entrance to New Harbor. Then the excitement began, first mildly and rather tentatively. Far yonder was unquestionably a little tower of spray, too slender to be made by a dashing wave, too transient to be confused with the smoke from a distant steamer. We headed eastward, leaving our course toward the harbor bell.

The occasional signs became unmistakable. One spout was less than a quarter of a mile away. Then, in a few moments, another. Anticipation was growing tense. We drew nearer. Ten or fifteen seconds after each water-spout we could make out a little black island which seemed to rise slowly above the surface, gradually revolving like the rim of an immense wheel and soon slowly disappearing.

Field glasses were trained on our game. Cameras were brought into action and triggers pulled. When these films are developed they will probably show that all we bagged was a dark speck on the watery horizon.

The game we were chasing soon disappeared and again we headed toward the harbor bell. Apparently this is precisely what the whales were doing too. Before long a spout was noted to the west, between us and the shore. It shot straight upward, but also moved forward along the surface while it lasted. Soon we saw several objects now and then rising like monster porpoises and for half a minute outlining their black backs against the glitter of the late afternoon sun. Twice we rounded the buoy. Evidently the whales were taking it easy not far distant. When one would appear we noted the direction of his slow progress and headed toward him, careful to set our course so that we would come astern of him rather than directly in his path.

The real adventure now began. We came close to the trail and lo! here were two Rorquals (finback whales, *Baleanoptera physalus*) almost side by side, slowly moving northward parallel with our course and distant scarcely three rods. My guess is that they were between fifty and sixty feet in length, although at no time did we see both head and tail. First to emerge was usually the top of the giant head, which then went down again as the smooth dark leathery shoulders and rounded back gradually came above the surface and moved forward in slow revolution until the triangular black dorsal fin was brought into view astern, and seemed to slide slowly along the arc of the black circle until it disappeared at the forward end of this arc. Rarely was any tail in evidence. This heavy member was kept well beneath the surface.

Before very long other whales were near. One of them was in a distinctly playful mood, rolling over on his back and showing first one and then the other of his pectoral flippers or fins, which were long, almost straight, and pointed so that they looked like slender spars when projecting six or eight feet above the surface. Once he thrust out his head in such a position that we could see the longitudinal folds of flesh on his whitish underjaw and throat, like a curiously striped and somewhat convex barn door—if you can picture such a thing.

A faithful phonograph would doubtless have recorded shouts and screams from each member of the crew. It would certainly have captured repeatedly the sound of blowing—like a locomotive standing in the railroad yards which suddenly has to let off steam.

We may have been in danger, but I don't think so. We offered no disturbance and were too trivial to be of the slightest concern to these vast mammals. Moreover, they were preoccupied with their own concerns. They were moving in pairs, close together. The leader of a pair was rarely as much as half a length ahead of her companion. Whenever she? rose into view, her mate was bound to show himself almost at the same instant.

At one time no less than three pairs were moving around our boat in this manner, like elephantine folk-dancers doing an infinitely slow and gracefully ponderous waltz, except that their evolutions, not limited to the two dimensions of a floor, revolved in three-dimensional twists and spirals. The climax came when one of these pairs appeared beside the boat less than two rods from our gunwales. They were so close that it seemed as though one might reach out with the boathook and tickle the offmember of the team.

As these conjugal play-mates disappeared from view, Roger Baldwin sank exhausted on a cushion in the cabin. He and all of us had reached the saturation point. Without reluctance we headed back toward Hog Island with a heavy cargo, not of baleen or of whaleoil, but of memories. . . .

As he staggered up our runway on his return, and before collapsing on the ground from sheer excitement, one of our guests described his terror when the side of a house, as he expressed it, suddenly loomed up from the deep right beside him. Not so Walter. He had been at the helm and was exhilarated by the thrill of a lifetime.

My mother's death in October, 1932, marked the end of the first part of our story. By that time my father was permanently disabled. I was their only child. The fate of our island was in my hands and I was deeply troubled for I feared I should have to let it go. I wrote: "When I walked through the woods and listened to the thrushes, the cry of the osprey circling overhead, or the boom of the great horned owl at night, I could never feel that I owned such a place. It seemed, rather, the property of all who cherished it and who wished to preserve it for others who would cherish it likewise in years to come. But that was hardly a practical point of view. So I began to wonder how I could make such a dream come true."

The story of the island's rescue has been told in the article already alluded to. What has not been told is that this would never have been possible had it not been for my husband's belief in the importance of my endeavor. For I was trying to find a way not only to save the island from the pulpwood industry, but to make it useful. It is true that the island itself gave me heart; but it was not the island only. Walter was there beside me to take my hand as we walked through the moss-carpeted forests or sat together on our pier beneath the stars on magic midsummer evenings, the tide at the full, the moon at the full. Talking of our plans, together we rowed out into the bay on dark silent nights when each stroke of the oars left a cloud of light deep down in the water, and ripples in the wake of the dory etched the surface with luminescence ploughed up from beneath, sparks on the surface blending with the reflected universe of stars.

Those were anxious times upon which it is not now necessary to dwell. During years of failure to rouse any person or any institution to the importance of preserving the island, Walter kept me from feeling discouraged. I knew that he did so not only because he wanted me to succeed in what I had undertaken, he realized also what this island properly administered could accomplish. That was the greatest help of all. And he was right. For success came at last and with it the third part of our story begins.

In June, 1936, as I have said, the Audubon Camp opened its doors. This is not the place in which to enumerate its accomplishments. That story must be told elsewhere. Under the leadership of Carl W. Buchheister who created it and, with the help of his superb staff, has directed it from the beginning, the Camp has become not only a source of delight and inspiration to us who are closest, its influence is felt far and wide throughout the nation. During the sixteen years since it started, with fifty students at a time for five two-week periods each summer, more than four thousand from forty-six states of the Union have come here to study the world of nature, the interconnections within it and related problems of conservation in this country. Here in the Audubon Camp, over the years, has been built up an esprit de corps so compelling that among the students differences of background, of education and of experience, as well as of age, are lost in a common enthusiasm. They have gained here a vision not only of the importance of an understanding of the world in which we live to find for themselves fullness of life; many of them leave with a sense of responsibility for arousing their communities to the urgent need of putting an end to the waste of our forests, grasslands, soil and water before it is too late.

But to return to the summer of 1936, an exciting adventure for us all. Not himself a student of nature, Walter's province was the naturalist or, as he said with an amused smile, observation of the birders, not the birds. While they studied the creatures in field or forest and the strange denizens of the deep, he studied them and gave a name, *Homo sapiens auduboniensis,* to this very special type of human being.

That summer he and I discovered that our professional interests crossed—mine in the out-of-doors, his in people.

Two aspects of the proposed program of instruction at the newly opened Camp impressed him for they had to do with fundamentals. First was the concept underlying all study of nature, namely, the resurgence of life from the products of death. Nothing is lost. This concept is as basic to an understanding of life on this planet as is that of the interdependence of everything that lives. Life is one— a fact obvious to anyone examining within a given area the relationships among living things which must depend one upon another out to the farthest filaments of their individual lives.

These principles are brought to the attention of the students at the Audubon Camp on the very first day. But they are not widely enough understood throughout the country. Walter had encountered at first hand the pioneer point of view, still too common in America, which countenances the reckless exploitation of our forests, our water and our soil. It has been our way to take what we want, leave the rest in ruins and move on to despoil the region next beyond, firm in our belief that there is always plenty more.

Equally important for the Camp, Walter felt, was another angle of approach to problems of conservation, one within his own field furthermore, the necessity of finding and training leaders for the out-of-doors occupations. Waste of talent in this country is only less distastrous than waste of natural resources. To help an able youth in the choice of a career nothing was too inconvenient for him to undertake. But, in parenthesis, it should be emphasized that Walter never *advised* anyone what to do. After a person's interests, aptitudes, skills and whatever else was measurable had been discovered, the results were placed before him; but the final decision as to choice of a career must be his own. "Here is where you stand among those who have succeeded in such and such an occupation," Walter would say. "But how much you *want* to enter it I cannot tell you. That makes all the difference," and he would quote Willa Cather: "If we could measure desire we could foretell achievement." Always my husband's main effort was to find ways of discovering talent at an early age, wherever it exists, at whatever level of society, in order to give it the chance to develop to the limit of its capacity. Only in this way, he felt, can leadership in a democracy be placed on a sound basis. And without proper leadership we cannot survive. So Walter had his own dream for the island too! Perhaps this search might be made an objective of the Audubon Camp—to help in finding leaders for such professions as forestry, soil conservation, wildlife management and so on. Those who come here, many of them in positions of influence in their various occupations, might be led to join in the hunt for such potential leaders among the young people of their own communities and to guide them toward a lifework which would give them not only scope for their abilities, but also the satisfaction of knowing that they are placed where they belong. If so, the fight for conservation in this country would be well served. With this objective in mind it did not take Walter long to decide what to do.

Soon after we left the island in the fall of 1936 he went about the task of planning in his usual systematic way. Among his notes made at that time I have found the draft of a letter to our friend Clark Wissler of the American Museum of Natural History.

Dear Dr. Wissler,

While combing through the scientific publications dealing with fundamental abilities and vocational interests, I have again and again been struck by the dearth of information about the abilities most needed in and the traits which have early characterized men who later have won distinction in the fields of the natural sciences. Precisely what signs of promise should we look for when awarding fellowships in the biological sciences, when choosing museum assistants, or when counseling with young people who are in doubt as to whether to direct their training toward a possible career in entomology, paleontology, ornithology, or forestry let us say, rather than toward chemistry or engineering, law or journalism, business, or one of the social service occupations?

To answer this question, the experience of those university professors and museum directors who have been more than ordinarily successful in discovering talent might well be brought together and consolidated. Personal data in the files of fellowship committees should be analyzed and compared with the subsequent records of the applicants. Biographical information regarding early interests and accomplishments of outstanding naturalists should also be sifted, in order to focus attention on differentiating traits.

It is not hard to imagine what some of these characteristics are: exceptional keenness in observation of detail; sensitivity to fine differences of form; fondness for the out-of-doors; love of wild life; interest in collecting, in classifying, in systematizing and in noting relationships; a penchant for clear inductive thinking, generalizing and rigorous verification; perhaps a concentration of interest and inclination within some specific area of inquiry. These and other traits instantly suggest themselves.

The problem has both scientific and practical bearings. Its study should result in isolating and defining certain primary abilities hitherto overlooked and at the same time should be of help in recognizing the symptoms of these abilities.

It has not been difficult to distinguish people whose bent is essentially mathematical or whose interests are in the physical sciences from those with marked linguistic talents, or from those whose abilities and tastes are essentially commercial, or artistic, or social. But no serious attempt has been made to define and specify the symptoms of superior promise of success in that large group of professions dealing primarily with the outdoor world of nature.

Do you think that some members of the staff of the American Museum of Natural History would be interested to collaborate in such an inquiry? ...

In this same folder there was a rough outline covering the entire field of aptitudes for the natural sciences as a major division of human occupations in the analysis of which Walter was at the time absorbed; for he was just finishing a book, *Aptitudes and Aptitude Testing,* published in 1937. A list of traits characteristic of the naturalist would, he hoped, provide a means for the early recognition of aptitudes for a lifework which, among designers of mental tests, I think he was first to recognize as a major profession. When I inquired whether an analysis of this field had ever been made before he replied, "Why—yes." "By whom?" I asked, "I hadn't heard of it." "By Aristotle," he said.

It was not long before Walter had an unexpected opportunity to present some of his findings. In October, 1937, he was asked to speak at the annual dinner of the Audubon Camp in the great Bird Hall of the American Museum of Natural History. What is said on such occasions is not usually of lasting value. But he could not let slip such an opportunity to pass along his thoughts by confining himself to a merely amusing after-dinner speech. So he concluded with a list of such traits as would be useful to the Audubon campers, teachers and others, in their search for future practitioners of natural science if I might call them such—the practical field workers.

At the end of the speech there was a moment of silence, after which applause echoed around the great Bird Hall as those present grasped the fact that they had received a gift of permanent value— a new tool for the early discovery of those who, in the open, will supervise the wise use of our basic resource—the land.

Only members of the Camp staff and students during the early years will recall some of the people and incidents mentioned. The migrant from the Bay of Whales, for instance, was Alton Lindsay, teacher of botany, who had accompanied Admiral Byrd on his second expedition. The voice from across the water at eventide belonged to the teacher of marine biology, "Jerry" Pomerat, whose command of utterance was not confined to Wagnerian melodies. And the voice of the common crow, heard each morning "about six o'clock," was that of Allan Cruickshank, who in those days waked the campers with his mimicry of the calls of certain birds. That was before the notes of the great bell boomed across the bay, now the signal not only for the campers but for those on the islands round about us, and for our neighbors on the nearby mainland, that another day is breaking. Allan's technique had its pitfalls however. One morning a conscientious teacher jumped out of bed before sunrise exclaiming to the dismay of her drowsy roommate, "Get up quick! Mr. Cruickshank just called!"—only to discover that she had heard a real crow.

During the years since 1937 Walter and I have often rowed across the bay to the Audubon Camp toward evening to meet a group of students fresh from a day of exploration in forest, field or marsh. After I had told them the story of the island he would read aloud *Homo sapiens auduboniensis.*

Those of us who gathered about him year after year on these memorable evenings will remember his voice, his courteousness and his amused comments on the incidents of long ago. Nor can we forget how intently he looked into the faces of those who, perhaps by the use of the tool he had fashioned, would be helped in identifying the young people best fitted to cope with urgent problems of the future. It might even be that in so doing they would help not only to preserve our land from further waste and destruction, but would also enable these same young people to find the lifework for which they themselves were best fitted and in the pursuit of which they would therefore find their greatest happiness and satisfaction. At any rate such was Walter Bingham's hope, and such because of him is our endeavor.

The speech follows just as Dr. Bingham gave it on October 22, 1937.

Preliminary Notes on Behavior and Ethology of Homo Sapiens Auduboniensis in the Muscongus Bay Region

OF all the forms of wild life for which the Todd Sanctuary on Hog Island provides a refuge, to me the most fascinating are not the baby Parula Warblers in their mossy nests, nor the soaring Ospreys, nor the Great Blue Heron, nor the fawns, not even the *Sciuridae,* but the primates. Here I have seen, for example, specimens of *Hominidae;* notably, in recent summers, flocks of the rare species *Homo sapiens Auduboniensis.*

What is this species like? How does it differ from other species of the genus *Homo?* What are its distinctive markings, its flight pattern, its song, its feeding habits, its behavior in caring for its young? How is it most readily distinguished from the birds of the vicinity with which it is often found in close association?

My notes suggest that in two respects *Auduboniensis* is strikingly like the Phalarope. Among the Phalaropes, which last summer visited Muscongus Bay literally by the thousands, you recall that it is the female which wears the brighter, more conspicuous plumage; also during courtship it is the female which makes the advances.

The song of the male *Auduboniensis* can easily be distinguished from that of the female. It is an octave lower in pitch and more robust in timbre. I have heard it often in the early morning, about 6 o'clock, at which time it sounds like that of the common Crow. Later in the day it resembles rather the chattering of Magpies, interspersed with cries like those made by the Laughing Gull; while at dusk it rivals the Hermit Thrush in lyric beauty and variety of melody.

One of their songs which last summer could be heard each evening toward sunset, punctually as the hoot of the Great Horned Owl, is like this: "O du mein holder Abendstern." Listeners with vivid imaginations have suggested that this song resembles a Wagnerian melody. On moonlit evenings *Audubonienses* could be heard singing in chorus, like bullfrogs. At such times their song sounds this way: "Good-night ladies." These unforgettable notes have a tender, plaintive quality when heard across the water, and indeed grow lovelier to the ear the more remote they are.

The habitat of *Auduboniensis* covers an almost unparalleled range. Specimens have been reported nesting as far north as Acadia, as far south as Florida, and as far west as the Pacific coast; while on Admiral Byrd's second expedition to the Antarctic, one migrant was seen in the Bay of Whales, in close association with a flock of Emperor Penguins—a bird to which the *Hominidae* are said to bear a curiously striking resemblance, not only in general appearance, but in their quaint manner of locomotion and solemn dignity of attitude. Like the Penguin, *Auduboniensis* cannot fly, but can ambulate rapidly over the land. It has been seen slowly and somewhat tentatively wading on mudflats, where it delves for worms. It is also at home in the water. Toward high noon its plumage sometimes undergoes a chameleon-like transformation, after which it utters a loud scream and plunges headlong into the sea.

The species is both herbivorous and carnivorous. It lives partly on the flesh of other vertebrates, partly on crustaceans, partly on seeds, fruits, and succulent herbs, but chiefly on an oleaginous, saccharine exudate of the *Theobroma cacao* known locally in Maine as chocolate bars.

Appearing as migrants during the summer months, as many

as fifty to sixty have been seen descending upon Hog Island in a single day. They were first observed in considerable numbers about June 9, 1936. Since that date they have often been noted, particularly on the northernmost point of the Island, and on the waters of Muscongus Bay. They have sometimes stayed within this area for two weeks, or even longer, before continuing their migration. Scarcely has one flock disappeared before another arrives, rapidly molting its spring plumage and appearing almost immediately in pin-feathers and down of variegated but unpredictable colors.

Of 223 specimens banded in 1936, 22 were observed again in the summer of 1937.

These migrants have been traced to remote parts of the country. Wherever found, it has been discovered that they behave like leaders among the *Hominidae* of their several localities. Many are engaged in care of the young, training them to act in an intelligent and friendly way toward other forms of wild life, for *Auduboniensis* seems to appreciate the mutual interdependence of different forms of life, and to understand the forces of the natural environments in which they thrive or perish.

It is obviously desirable that more and more *Audubonienses* should, in future summers, find their way to the Todd Wildlife Sanctuary. But since the environment there has only a limited coverage for protecting them from predators and storms, the wardens of this sanctuary must take steps to see that these haunts are not appropriated by other species of *Hominidae*. I am especially apprehensive of the *Summer-vacationistoria,* partly because this less active and more self-indulgent species is not always easy to distinguish from the true *Auduboniensis*. And so I shall try to describe more precisely the distinctive characteristics of this latter species.

It must be confessed that I have had to abandon all attempts to identify *Auduboniensis* by its plumage alone, or its form, or its external markings. It can be recognized only by its behavior.

1. *Auduboniensis* exhibits, while still immature, a strong preference for woods, marshes, streams, prairies, wilderness—in other words, for the out-of-doors. (This trait persists into maturity, instead of dying out as it does with many other species of *Homo*.)

2. It is not to be deterred from its pursuits by discomforts and difficulties—by mosquitoes or swamps or storms.

3. It exhibits an absorbing curiosity regarding certain forms of vegetation and wild life. It watches them closely, and examines them in great detail.

4. It is peculiarly sensitive to the beauty and the worth of different forms of life. It cherishes them.

5. It gathers and brings to its lair choice specimens of certain forms, but not if these forms are rare or in danger of extinction.

6. It excels in ability to observe slight differences among these forms: differences of color, of sound, of size and shape; differences of markings, texture, pattern; differences of behavior.

7. It can describe these differences accurately with words, or pencil, or brush, or camera.

8. It also excels in noting similarities, even though these similarities may be obscure. In other words, it has highly developed powers of observing, classifying, abstracting and generalizing; that is, an aptitude for scientific thinking.

9. Its curiosity extends to questions of relationships between different forms of life and the connections between events. It is a rational animal, with a strong proclivity for exercising its mind on problems presented by the world of nature.

10. But it is capable of retaining, in the presence of nature, an attitude of wonder.

These ten characteristics seem to be peculiarly in evidence

among naturalists, young and old. Those who most greatly benefit their species are endowed with yet another characteristic—
the capacity to make their interests and enthusiasms contagious.

These are the leaders. It is primarily to shelter and to encourage such potential leaders that the Audubon Nature Camp exists. It is our privilege to discover them when we can, and to stimulate their flight in the direction of Muscongus Bay.

This preliminary report of observations on the characteristics of nature students has been offered, not only because the natural history of the *Hominidae* is in itself a topic of absorbing interest, but more especially because this particular species, *Auduboniensis,* plays a vital rôle in the great drama of conservation. Before many years have passed it will be recognized as performing one of the key functions in maintaining the balance of nature on this continent.

Epilogue

Walter Bingham's life-interest focused on the identification of potential leaders as early in life as possible or, as a fellow-psychologist phrased it, on "the discovery and encouragement of professional talent." In an autobiographical sketch published shortly after his death, Dr. Bingham says of this predilection of his that it is "but one manifestation of a dominant purpose, namely, to invest my energies in helping the well-adjusted to achieve their fullest usefulness. I have preferred to give a hand to the promising rather than to the weak, the unhappy, the unadjusted, whom we psychologists may wisely leave, whenever we can, to the ministration of our friends, the psychiatrists and the social workers. We should thank them for their willingness to relieve us of all responsibility for therapy, thereby freeing the psychological profession for the more congenial and, I sincerely believe, more socially useful task of augmenting the productivity and the happiness of the mentally well."

Dr. Bingham's influence has been widely recognized in the growing realization, not only in science but in education, in government and in other fields, that unless the able and talented can be found in their youth, freed, and given the opportunity to develop their powers to the limit of their ability, our country will lack the guidance requisite for its newly-assumed rôle of leadership in world affairs.

In a mechanized society the sciences whose applications are of most immediate practical use have fared best in the search for talent which has been going on for some time. But Dr. Bingham felt that it has not been comprehensive enough. The following letter gives evidence not only of his preoccupation with this subject as related to the discovery of leaders in the field of conservation of our natural resources, but also —a fact which touches us even more closely—with his deep and continuing interest in the activities of the Audubon Camp of Maine.

C. W. B.

1661 *Crescent Place*
Washington 9, *D. C.*
September 21, 1948

Mr. *Carl Buchheister*
National Audubon Society
1000 *Fifth Avenue*
New York, N. Y.

Dear Carl:

You would have been interested in one of the *AAAS* Centennial meetings last week, a symposium on discovery and development of scientific talent. They were appraising the results of the Westinghouse Awards in the annual Science Talent Search among high school seniors.

I checked up on the professions which the two hundred odd winners have chosen to enter. More than three-fourths of them have headed into physics, chemistry, mathematics, or engineering; less than one-fourth have gone in for biology, botany, forestry, entomology, agriculture, medicine, bacteriology, or any other field concerned with living organisms. As a people we are evidently continuing to emphasize and honor machinery and the physical sciences, although it should be evident to everyone that what the world needs most is not so much another surge of mechanical inventions or atomic discoveries, but brilliant advances in the life sciences without which our wonderful mechanisms and bombs will probably put an end to contemporary civilization if not to the human race.

I drew the attention of the symposium to the small number of Talent Search winners who, in choosing a "project" to submit in the national competition, had offered a study having to do with living things: insects, rodents, weeds, birds, fertility, or what have you. The proportion was about one in four. I then reminded them that many of the great naturalists had, by the time they were twelve years old, already acquired an absorbing interest in the field in which they later made their famous contributions.

This cleared the decks, and I wound up by reminding them of the central purpose of the Audubon Nature Camp: to equip teachers and youth leaders with the determination *and the* skills *with which to focus the interests of youngsters on some aspect of our natural resources before they have outgrown this crucially decisive phase of mental development.*

Speakers who followed, including several who knew about the Camp and its accomplishments, took off from one or more of the points I had emphasized.

A Miss Cook (or Cooke) who spoke to me afterwards, undertook to match my expressions of admiration for what one Carl Buchheister has accomplished.

With warm regards, as always,

WALTER V. BINGHAM